. . . you don't
want it to

. . . it's during Johnny Carson

. . . it's for personal research

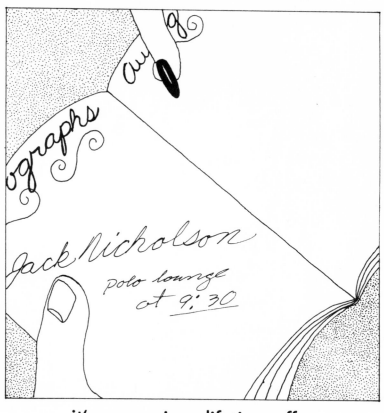

. . . it's a once-in-a-lifetime offer

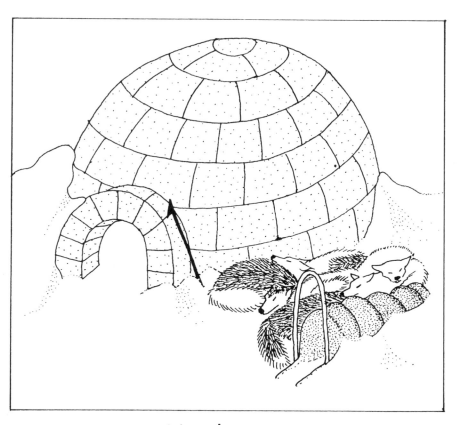

. . . it's to keep warm

. . . c'est pour montrer que vous n'avez
aucun préjugé

. . . quiere demostrar que usted es sin
prejuicio

( . . . it's to show you're not prejudiced)

ZZZZ ZZZZZZ ZZZZZZZ

. . . you don't
wake up

it's for revenge

November. . .

October. . .

September. . .

. . . it's your bridal shower

. . . you're     inter rupted

. . . you're serving your country

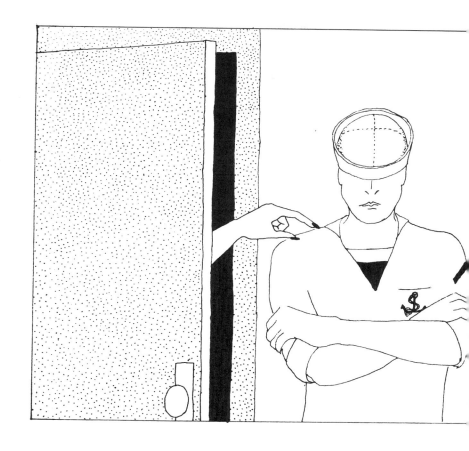

. . . you're just trying to firm up your

# THIGHS

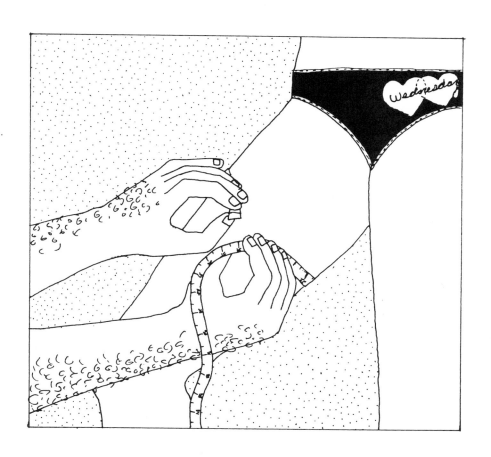

...you're **P**regnant

. . . there are more than five involved

...you'll never see
him again

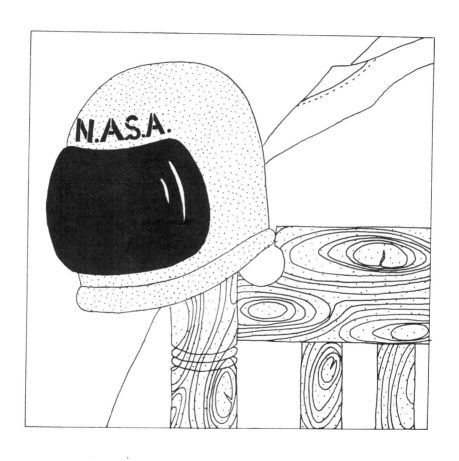

. . . he's going off to

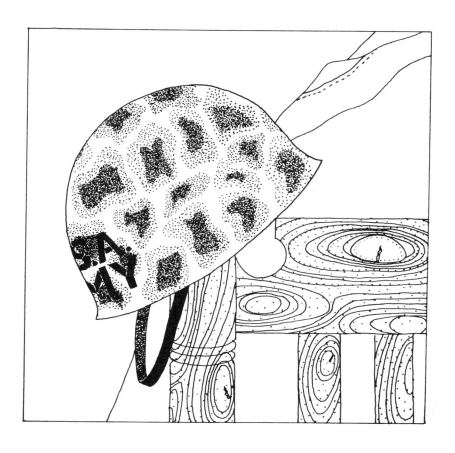

*Diploma*

. . . he's going off to college

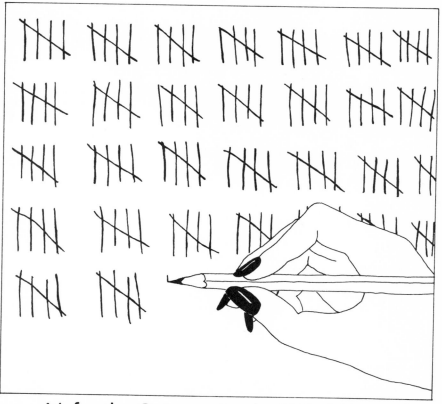

. . . it's for the *Guinness Book of World Records*

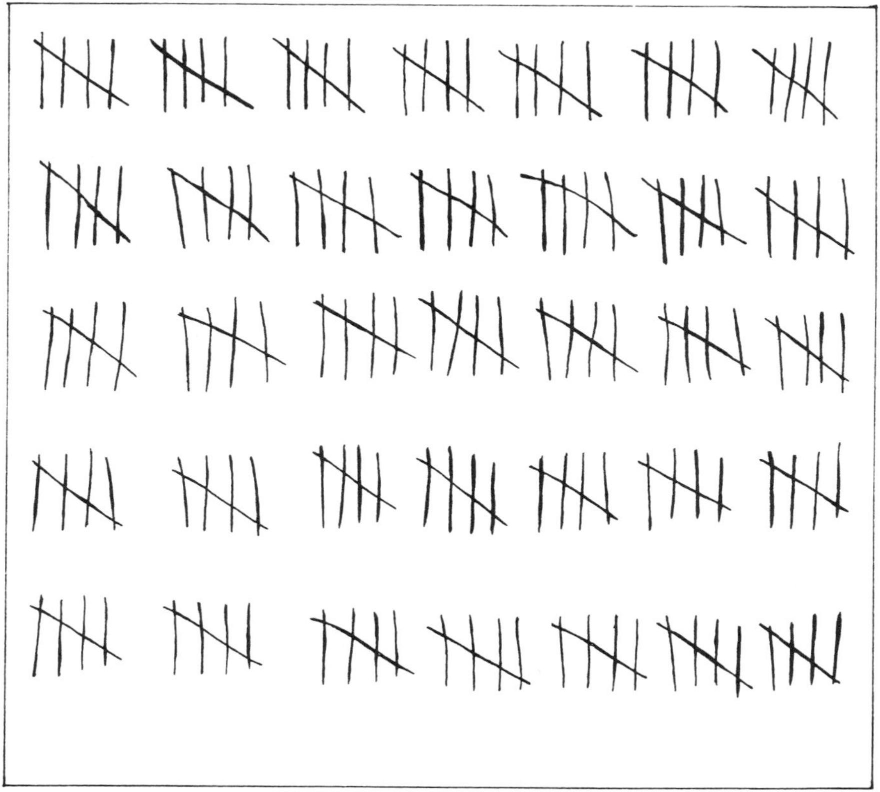

. . . it's your last day on earth

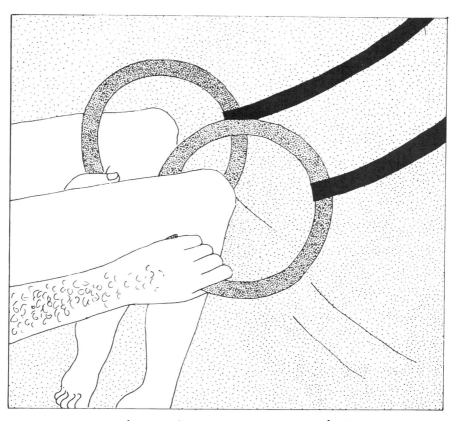

. . . you're trying out a new technique

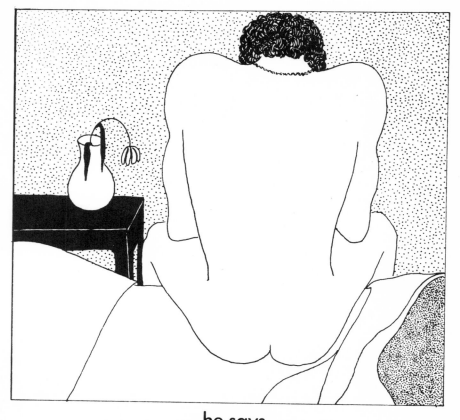

. . . he says,
"I'm sorry, this has never happened to me before."

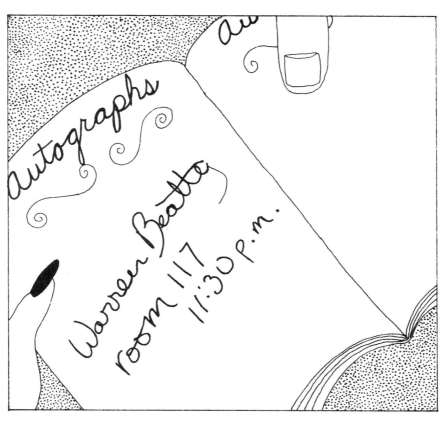

. . . it's a once-in-a-lifetime offer

...you're
making
a movie

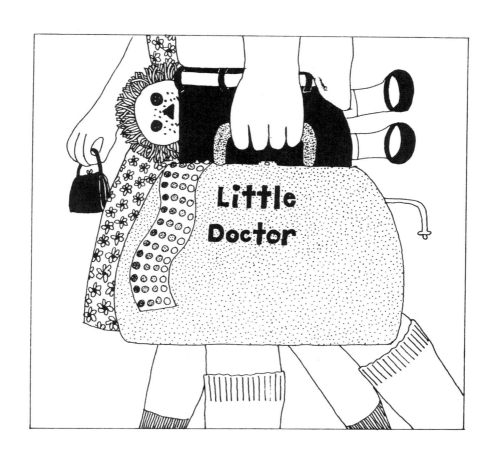

. . . you don't speak the same language

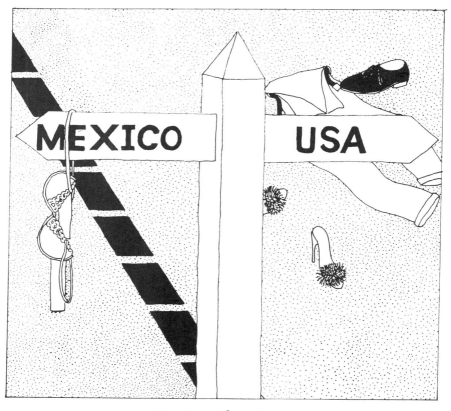

. . . you're in a foreign country

DIVORCE DECREE

YOU USED TO BE MARRIED TO HIM

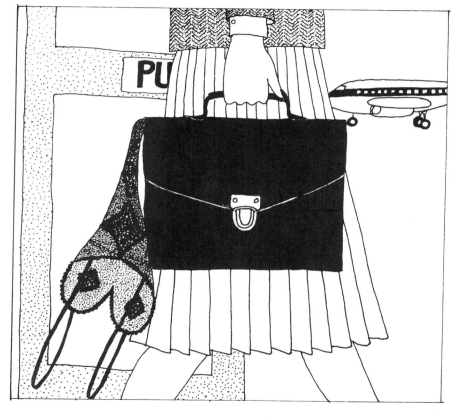

. . . you're out of town

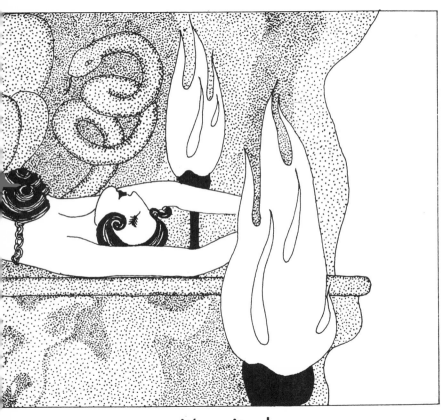

. . . it's a ritual

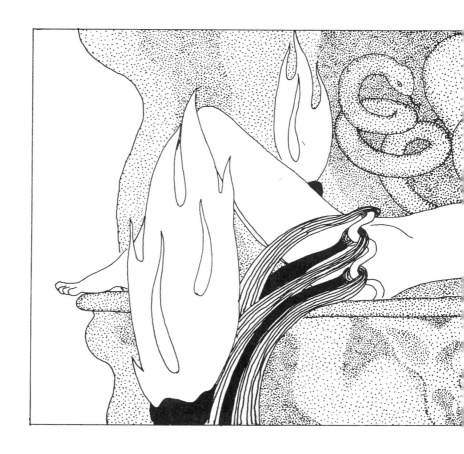

. . . he has a
terminal
illnes s

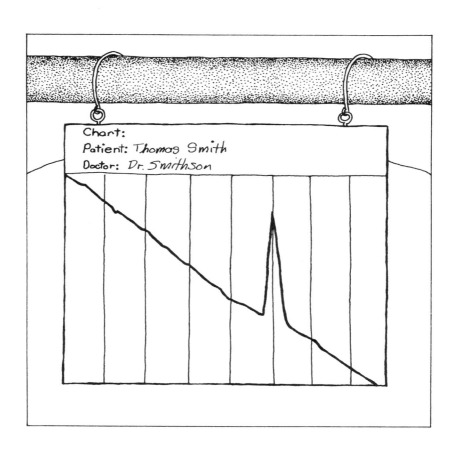

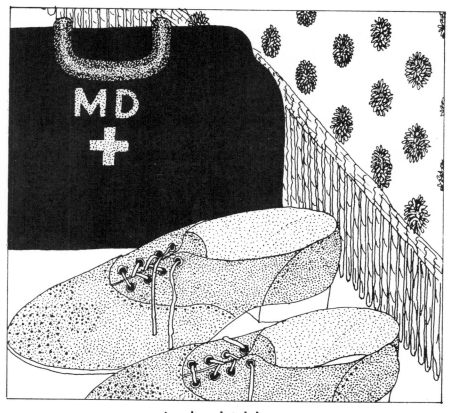

. . . you're bedridden anyway

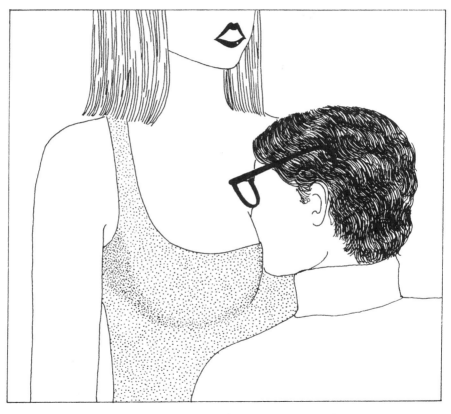

. . . you weren't expecting it

*...he's gone to all that trouble*

. . . it's for old times' sake

. . . you don't put your book down

. . . or after . . . a

# NATURAL DISASTER

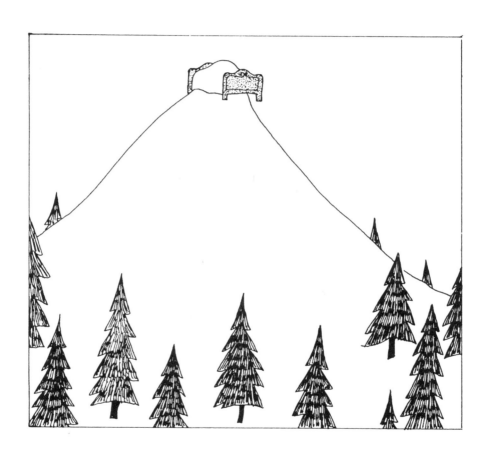

. . . during . . .

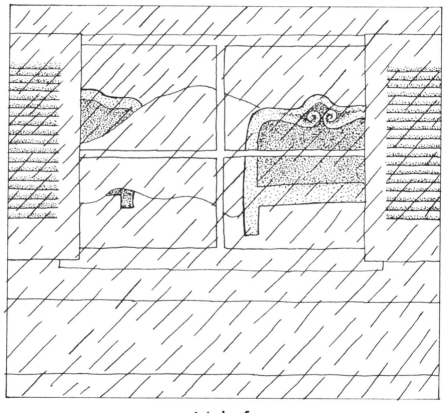

. . . it's before

. . . you don't
use your
hands

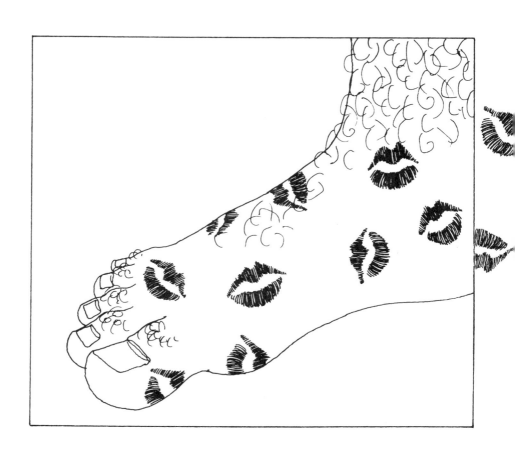

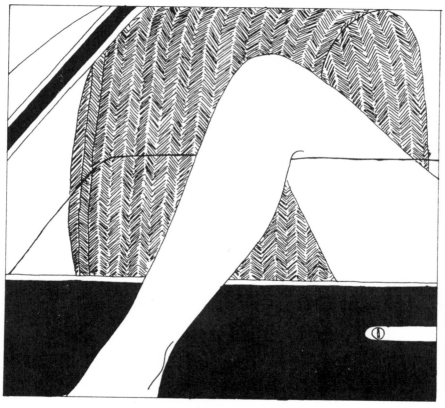

. . . you're in an MG

. . . you feel sorry for him

Hotel Register

John Doe          anytown, USA
Joe Smith                      "
Bill Jones        "            "
John Smith        "            "
Bill Doe          "            "
Joe Jones         "            "
John Doe          "            "
Joe Smith         "            "
Bill Jones        "            "
John Smith        "            "

. . . you don't know his name

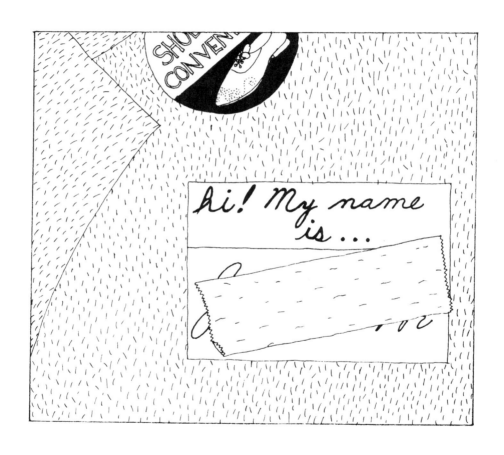

. . . there's n◯thing

else to do

. . . you don't take your clothes off

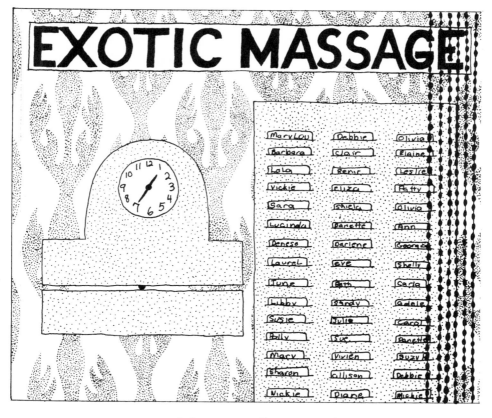

. . . it's part of your job

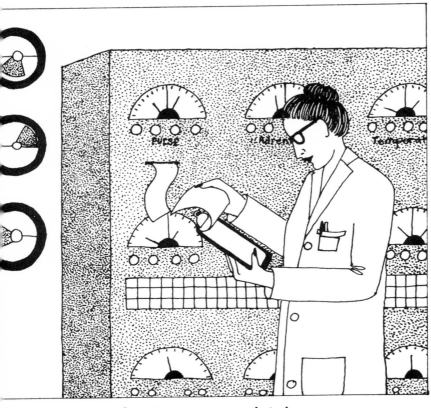

. . . it's for Masters and Johnson

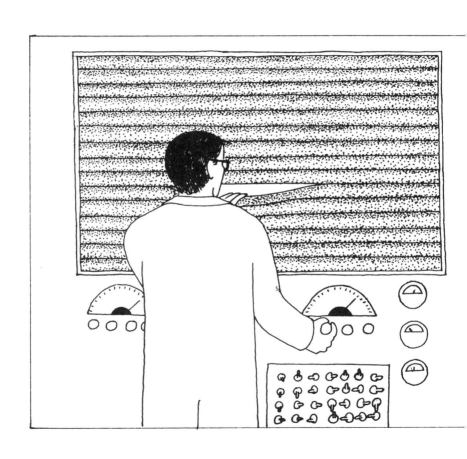

. . . you're saving
him from
homosexuality

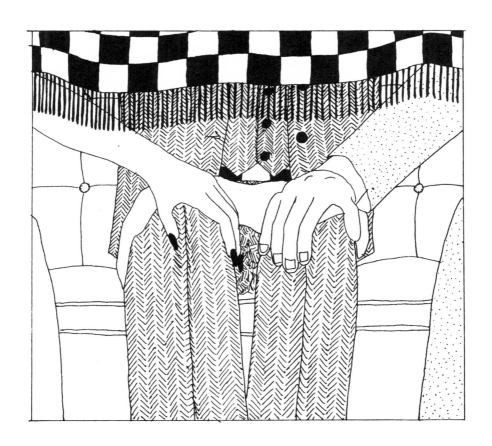

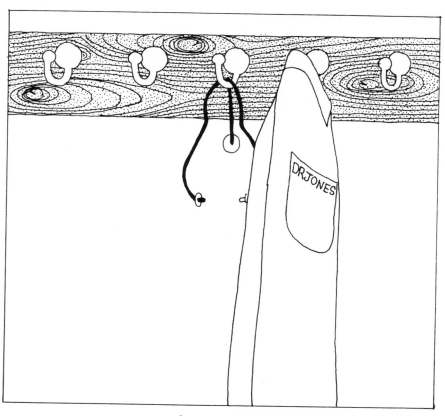

. . . your mother approves of him

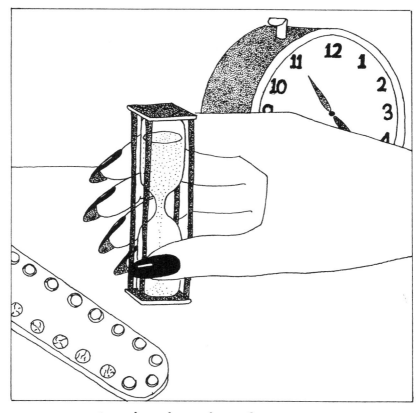

. . . it takes less than five minutes

. . . you're at the Club Med

. . . you had too much to drink

. . . it's a once-in-a-lifetime offer

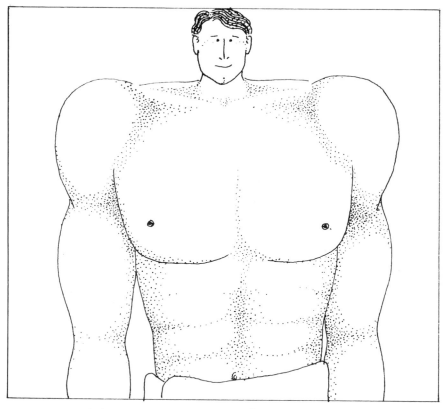

. . . it's not a "meaningful" relationship

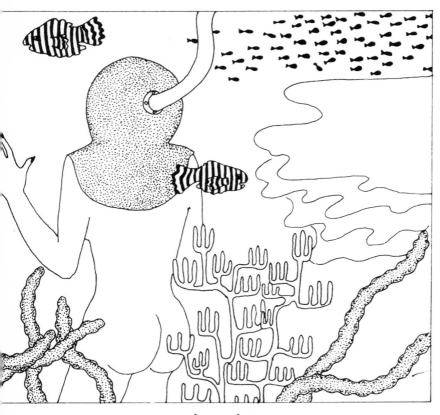

. . . you don't kiss

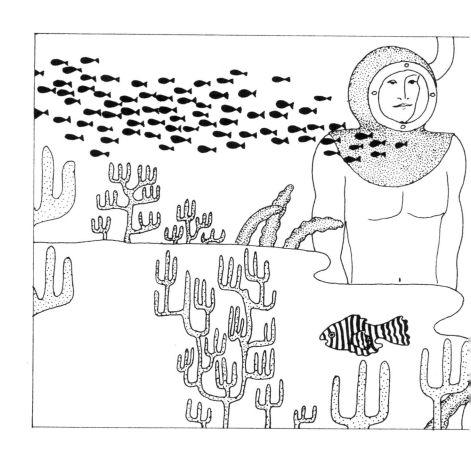

. . . you keep
one foot on the floor

.

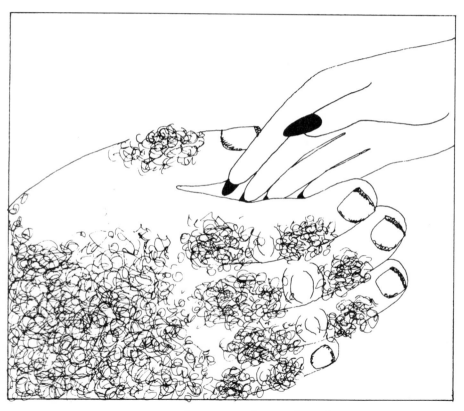

. . . you're doing a friend a favor

## Disclaimer to My Mother

None of the information contained in this book comes from first-hand knowledge. Rather, it was all gathered from years of arduous library research and from the most reliable sources—such as whispered conversations overheard in the Palm Court at the Plaza, quick exchanges in the powder rooms of chic discotheques, tear-stained pages fallen out of friends' personal diaries, the yellowed pages of old articles in *Cosmo*, fresh translations of the ancient graffiti on Caligula's Baths, and, of course, the personal surveys conducted by my more-experienced neighbor across the hall.

So you see, Mom, there is certainly none of me in this. I simply offer my findings to whatever use the reader may wish to put them.

*Sara Parriott*

## Acknowledgments

I owe a debt of gratitude to a number of people, but most specifically to my publisher, Jeremy Tarcher, my editor, Victoria Pasternack, my publicist, Lucinda Dyer, and certainly not least, my invaluable counselor and advisor, Mary Lou Brady, without whose help this book would not have been possible.

**Dedicated to**
Alvin
Bruce
Cliff
Dave
Eddie
Frank
George
Hal
Irving
Jacques
Kurt
Len
Mitch
Norm
Oscar
Pete
Quentin
Ralph
Sidney
Tod
Umberto
Vic
Wally
Xeno
Yves
Zach
and to those whose names are long forgotten     Just thanks.

Copyright © 1979 by Sara Parriott
All rights reserved.
Library of Congress Catalog Card No.: 79-66310
Distributor's ISBN: 0-312-90857-1
Publisher's ISBN: 0-87477-113-7
Design by Educational Graphics
Manufactured in the United States of America
Published by J.P. Tarcher, Inc.
9110 Sunset Blvd., Los Angeles, Calif. 90069
Published simultaneously in Canada by Thomas Nelson & Sons Limited,
81 Curlew Drive, Don Mills, Ontario M3A 2R1
10   9   8   7   6   5   4   3   2   1
First Edition

# Sex Doesn't Count When . . .

. . . you don't wake up

## Sara Parriott

J.P. Tarcher, Inc., Los Angeles
Distributed by St. Martin's Press, New York